TEXAS GEOGRAPHY

Michael Rajczak

New York

Published in 2014 by The Rosen Publishing Group, Inc.
29 East 21st Street, New York, NY 10010

Copyright © 2014 by The Rosen Publishing Group, Inc.

Book Design: Mickey Harmon

Photo Credits: Cover (Texas) Map Resources/Shutterstock.com; cover (plains) Somer McCain/Shutterstock.com;
cover (mountains) Rusty Dodson/Shutterstock.com; cover (beach) urbanlight/Shutterstock.com; pp. 4, 10 RIRF
Stock/Shutterstock.com; p. 5 (prickly pear) Bill Florence/Shutterstock.com; p. 5 (yucca) cameilia/
Shutterstock.com; p. 5 (cactus) Curioso/Shutterstock.com; p. 5 (juniper) Jiinna/Shutterstock.com;
p. 5 (lechuguilla) Stan Shebs/Wikipedia.org; p. 5 (tobosa grass) Robert Soreng, Smithsonian Institution/fd.fed.
gov; p. 5 (armadillo) Heiko Kiera/Shutterstock.com; p. 5 (roadrunner) Jason Mintzer/Shutterstock.com;
p. 5 (collared peccary) Shane Kennedy/Shutterstock.com; p. 5 (coyote) Geoffrey Kuchera/Shutterstock.com;
p. 5 (snake) Kuznetsov Alexey/Shutterstock.com; p. 5 (lizard) Jeremy Woodhouse/Photodisc/Getty Images;
p. 7 gary yim/Shutterstock.com; p. 9 Brandon Seidel/Shutterstock.com; p. 11 Becky Sheridan/Shutterstock.
com; pp. 12–13 Frontpage/Shutterstock.com; p. 14 Mike McMurray/Shutterstock.com; p. 15 Jeffrey M. Frank/
Shutterstock.com; pp. 16, 17 Leaflet/Wikipedia.org; p. 18 Sergio Schnitzler/Shutterstock.com; p. 19 cholder/
Shutterstock.com; p. 20 iStockphoto/Thinkstock.com; p. 21 mikenorton/Shutterstock.com; p. 23 Natalia
Bratslavsky/Shutterstock.com; p. 24 Jim Parkin/Shutterstock.com; p. 25 (Rayburn Reservoir) Mrrightguy10/
Wikipedia.org; p. 25 (Lake Texoma) Jpowersok/Wikipedia.org; p. 27 Berry, Kelley & Chadwick/Library of Congress;
p. 29 (sunset) Willard Clay/Photographer's Choice/Getty Images; p. 29 (inset) spirit of america/Shutterstock.com.

Library of Congress Cataloging-in-Publication Data

Rajczak, Michael.
Texas geography / by Michael Rajczak.
 p. cm. — (Spotlight on Texas)
Includes index.
ISBN 978-1-4777-4533-5 (pbk.)
ISBN 978-1-4777-4534-2 (6-pack)
ISBN 9978-1-4777-4532-8 (library binding)
1. Texas — Geography — Juvenile literature. 2. Texas — Juvenile literature. I. Rajczak, Michael. II. Title.
F386.8 R33 2014
917.64—dc23

Manufactured in the United States of America

CPSIA Compliance Information: Batch #WW14RC: For further information contact Rosen Publishing, New York, New York at 1-800-237-9932.

CONTENTS

TEXAS BY THE NUMBERS

The state of Texas is a beautiful place with a wide variety of interesting geographical features. From sea level at the Gulf of Mexico to Guadalupe Peak at 8,749 feet (2,667 m) above sea level, you could spend a lifetime exploring all the valleys, rivers, hills, and prairies Texas has to offer.

Texas is the second-largest state in the United States, covering 268,601 square miles (695,677 sq km). It has a unique puzzle-piece shape bordered by New Mexico to the west and Oklahoma to the north. It shares an eastern border with Arkansas and Louisiana. To the south, the Rio Grande forms the 1,255-mile (2,019 km) border between Texas and Mexico. Texas also boasts 350 miles (563 km) of coastline along the Gulf of Mexico. Because of its size and geography, Texas has a wide variety of animals, plants, and climates.

The Rio Grande became the Texas-Mexico border at the end of the Mexican-American War in 1848.

prickly pear cactus
(official state plant)

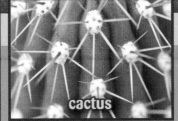
cactus

yucca

juniper

lechuguilla

tobosa grass

PLANTS

IN THE DESERT

ANIMALS

armadillo
(official state animal)

roadrunner

collared peccary
(javelina)

coyote

snake

Texas horned lizard

Texas has a reputation for being a dry and dusty place, but the fact is that less than 10 percent of the state is actually considered desert! Still, many desert symbols are associated with Texas.

BEFORE THE EUROPEANS

Before Spanish explorers and settlers came to Texas, several Native American groups lived as hunters and gatherers in the state's diverse environments. However, the Caddo Confederacy established villages in Texas's eastern Piney Woods region. Here, forests were a source of building materials and wild game. The **bayous** and rivers were excellent sources of freshwater and fish. The Caddos also farmed many traditional crops such as corn, beans, squash, and tobacco.

Outside this region, Texas was a dry, forbidding landscape. Away from the rivers and few lakes, cacti and tumbleweeds covered the land. Bison roamed freely in the central basin regions. Bighorn sheep, deer, coyotes, and bears lived in the forests and highlands. The untouched natural beauty of mountains and rocky **escarpments** posed big challenges to the first European explorers in Texas.

Before Spanish explorers arrived, herds of bison provided resources for Native Americans on the Texas plains.

COASTAL PLAINS

Two-thirds of Texas's population lives in the eastern part of the state, which is known as the coastal plains region. This includes the land that rises from the Gulf of Mexico up to about 500 feet (152 m) above sea level. To the south is the Rio Grande, which forms the border with Mexico. To the north, you'll find the Red River, which borders Oklahoma. The coastal plains' eastern border is shared with Arkansas and Louisiana.

Many large cities are found in this region, including Houston, Brownsville, Laredo, Corpus Christi, Huntsville, Beaumont, Tyler, and Longview. Austin, the state's capital, and San Antonio are on the western edge of the coastal plains. Padre Island, Galveston Island, and other barrier islands are just off the Texas coast. The islands provide some protection from tropical storms coming in from the Gulf of Mexico.

Texas's capital city, which was named after Stephen F. Austin, was established on the banks of the Colorado River.

Austin, Texas

The coastal plains region is known for its rich soil. A wide variety of citrus fruits and vegetables is grown here, in addition to cotton and grain. However, the grasslands make it hard to grow much rice and wheat. This region's gentle slopes and flat fields support the raising of livestock such as cattle, pigs, sheep, and horses.

The northern coastal plains have pine and oak trees, but you can see palm trees in the south as the climate grows warmer. Here, the climate is humid and **subtropical**, with blistering heat in the summer months. This area of Texas receives the greatest amount of rainfall since it's next to the Gulf of Mexico. As a result, tropical storms and hurricanes tend to occur in this region. Yearly precipitation rates vary, and even with modern irrigation, **drought** conditions can last for several seasons at a time.

These trees are just one example of the natural beauty seen throughout Texas.

Mountains and Basins

West Texas is known for its mountains and basins. This area has very hot summers and dry winters. The mountains and basins region is bordered by New Mexico to the north and by Mexico and the Rio Grande to the south and west. The Pecos River runs through this region's eastern portion. Forests of pine trees similar to those in the Rocky Mountains exist in the north, while vast deserts exist in the southernmost part. The population is scarce and scattered in these areas.

Texas's only true mountains are in this region; there are several peaks that reach 7,000 feet (2,134 m) or higher! The Franklin Mountains tower over the large city of El Paso, which has over 1 million people in its **metropolitan** area. The city is within the Chihuahuan Desert, although intense summer thunderstorms sometimes cause flooding.

People adapted to west Texas's rugged geography and created the city of El Paso beneath the Franklin Mountains.

West Texas's dry climate and rugged geography have greatly affected the economy of the mountains and basins region. The Permian Basin area is famous for its oil and natural gas fields. The area is also known for mining rock salt and minerals used for making **fertilizer**. There are also several areas with enough soil for grasslands. There, you can find herds of cattle and goats. With few homes and trees to break the wind, people have created wind farms that use hundreds of windmills to produce electricity.

Western Texas receives the lowest amount of rain in the state. However, grain and cotton crops are still grown here. Many of these crops help feed the more populated areas of Fort Stockton, Odessa, and Midland. Since water is scarce, west Texans drill wells to tap into an **aquifer**. Over 70 percent of the water used to irrigate crops comes from this source.

Wind energy is good for the environment because it doesn't cause pollution.

The Permian Basin

Have you ever heard of the Permian Basin? It's a flat area of rock in the center of a geographical ring formed by the Guadalupe Mountain Range, the Apache Mountains, and the Glass Mountains in Texas. This part of Texas's landscape has one of the world's thickest deposits of rock from the Permian geological period. That's how it got its name.

This flat basin is mostly made of limestone with brightly colored shale. Long ago, the mountains surrounding it were once part of an underwater **reef**. Visitors can find an abundance of marine fossils in the area, including plant life, reptiles, and mammal-like reptiles. The Central Basin Platform, Marfa Basin, and sediment-filled Midland Basin are also parts of the Permian Basin.

NORTH CENTRAL PLAINS

The center of northern Texas that borders Oklahoma along the Red River is known as the north central plains. The rolling prairies and hills that begin at the edge of the coastal plains mark the beginning of this region. Its elevation begins at about 1,000 feet (305 m) above sea level and gradually increases to over 3,000 feet (914 m) in the west at the Caprock Escarpment.

This rise of hardpan rock forms a natural boundary between the central plains area and the high plains Panhandle region. Summers are humid and subtropical, but mild winters sometimes bring icy blasts from the North. This region sees its share of tornadoes and hailstorms, too. Though Native American tribes lived here, no one group dominated this area. It had a series of trails used by several tribes. Today, Dallas, Fort Worth, Abilene, and Wichita Falls are the region's most populated cities.

The Caprock Escarpment was formed about 1 million to 2 million years ago.

There are several rivers in the north central plains region, including the Trinity, the Brazos, and the Wichita Rivers. However, much of the water used in this area comes from underground aquifers. The area's major cities—Dallas, Fort Worth, and Arlington (together known as the Metroplex)—are growing, leading many people to believe water sources could run out one day.

Before the Civil War, cotton plantations along the Trinity River were a booming business in central Texas. Today, cotton remains a key crop, along with wheat, peanuts, and grain **sorghum**. Cattle are raised for dairy and beef production.

sorghum field

The raising of livestock such as chickens, hogs, sheep, and goats continues rural traditions on both large and small family farms. Many large ranches in this region are dedicated to breeding some of the finest horses in the nation. Most of the coal mined in Texas comes from the north central plains area. As a result, natural gas is also collected here.

cotton field

Sorghum and cotton thrive on farms in central Texas.

GREAT PLAINS

The "Panhandle" is the nickname for Texas's northernmost area. This region is the southern part of the vast Great Plains, which go all the way to Canada. The Panhandle is narrow and straight on three sides. When viewed on a map, the state looks like a pan with a short handle sticking up. That's where the nickname comes from.

Almost 25 percent of this region is completely flat, making it one of the largest flat areas in the world. This flat area is known as the Staked Plains, or *Llano Estacado*. The area is also home to rolling hills, where elevation increases from about 2,000 feet (610 m) above sea level in the southeast corner to over 4,700 feet (1,433 m) in the northwest. The southern portion of the region is the Edwards Plateau. The eastern part of the plateau is known as Hill Country because of its many steep hills. Northwest of the Edwards Plateau is the Toyah Basin, which is an ancient seabed of the Pecos River valley.

Windmills that help pump water dot the
Texas Panhandle landscape.

The Grand Canyon of Texas

The Palo Duro Canyon is a canyon system in the Texas Panhandle, located just 27 miles (43 km) southeast of Amarillo. It's second only to the Grand Canyon in size, and the views from this location are spectacular. The canyon was formed millions of years ago from **erosion** by the Red River. The view from the rim is breathtaking.

Palo Duro Canyon is roughly 60 miles (97 km) long and spans 20 miles (32 km) across at its widest point. It's about 820 feet (250 m) deep in most places, but it dips to 997 feet (304 m) at its deepest point.

Early Spanish explorers gave the area its name, which means "hard wood" in English. This refers to the many juniper and mesquite trees in and around the canyon. Camping, horseback riding, and studying nature are popular activities in this area.

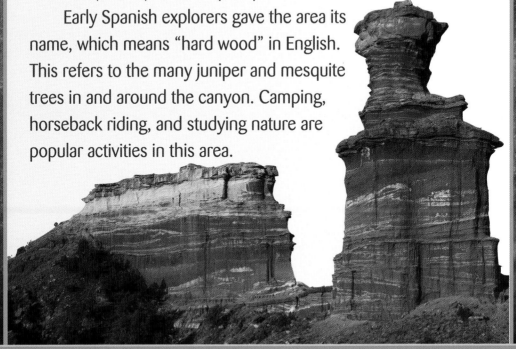

In 1541, explorer Francisco Vázquez de Coronado referred to Texas's Great Plains area as a "sea of grass." The amount of grass made it a perfect place for wild cattle to graze. Eventually, long cattle drives began from this region. Cattle ranching and farming are still the area's major sources of business. Wheat, sorghum, and cotton are also harvested here.

Population centers grew along this region's reliable sources of freshwater, such as the Red, Colorado, and Brazos Rivers. Today, aquifers provide more water for ranches, farms, and towns. The plains region boasts two larger cities, Amarillo and Lubbock, with Plainview located between them. Most of the world's **helium** supply comes from the area around Amarillo.

The Great Plains region has drier and cooler summers than the coastal areas, and because of the elevation, winters are cold. Violent storms, such as the devastating tornado that hit Lubbock in 1970, are known to impact the Great Plains region.

This cotton is ready for harvest near Lubbock, Texas.

WATER: THE MOST IMPORTANT RESOURCE

Water has always affected how Texas was settled. People tended to settle along freshwater rivers and areas with natural harbors and access to the Gulf of Mexico. This was true of Native American groups and later true for European settlers. Freshwater was essential for drinking and irrigating crops. Access to the gulf encouraged trade. The need for sources of freshwater increased as more settlers came, so Texans turned to digging and drilling for water.

Today, water management affects every citizen in Texas. Drought conditions can last several years. From clearing land of plants that soak up water to limiting how often residents can water their lawns or wash their cars, the goal is always to preserve water resources. As the water levels in aquifers and reservoirs become strained and the population continues to grow, Texans will continue to look for new sources of freshwater.

Drier areas in Texas depend on irrigation to water their crops.

Texas's Man-Made Lakes

Lake Conroe (near Houston)

Sam Rayburn Reservoir (north of Beaumont)

Lake Texoma (northwest of Denison)

Lake Tawakoni (southeast of Greenville)

Cedar Creek Lake (southeast of Dallas)

Canyon Lake (near San Antonio)

Lake Fort Worth (in Fort Worth city limits)

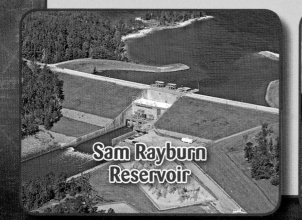
Sam Rayburn Reservoir

Lake Texoma

Believe it or not, most of Texas's lakes are man-made.
They bring drinking water, water for farming, and
recreational opportunities to Texans around the state.

Geography and Texas History

The Mexican-American War (1846–1848) is an important part of Texas's history. One of the war's causes was a dispute over which river formed Texas's southern boundary. The United States considered the Rio Grande as the southern border, but Mexico claimed it was the more northern Nueces River.

Later, in 1874, the Palo Duro Canyon became a battle site during the Red River War. The canyon's walls allowed the United States Army to trap the Comanche tribes and their 1,400 horses who lived there. Also in the 1870s, Charles Goodnight began using the canyon as a corral for his herd of over 100,000 longhorn cattle.

Texas's southern location caused cotton plantations to develop throughout the state. This made slavery an important part of Texas's economy in the 1800s. During this same era, many Texans felt the federal government did not do enough to protect them from Native Americans and Mexican bandits. These two reasons caused Texas to join other Southern states in **seceding** from the Union in 1861.

Texas's landscape was dotted with many cotton plantations, which led to the growth of slavery in the state.

A Land of Contrasts

Texas is referred to as a land of contrasts because of all the different geographical features found throughout the state. Beaches can be found along the Gulf of Mexico, from Brownsville to Galveston. In the northwestern part of the state, the foothills of the Rocky Mountains make skiing and snowboarding popular activities. In between, time seems to stand still in wide-open spaces where few people have ever been. There are big cities with big universities, state-of-the-art transportation, and professional sports and entertainment, but also small communities where everyone knows each other's name.

Texans sometimes shape the environment, such as when they create lakes or manage soil resources. But Mother Nature has yet to be tamed—just look at Texas's droughts and hurricanes as proof. However, no matter where you go in Texas, there's always something new and interesting to discover about its beautiful geography.

Texas geography varies from the beautiful beaches on Padre Island to the jagged peaks of its mountains.

READER RESPONSE PROJECTS

- Each region of Texas has many exciting and interesting qualities. Pick the region you're most interested in. Use this book, the Internet, and other resources to learn more about it. Make an informational poster or a computer presentation to teach your friends and classmates about this area's interesting geography.

- As you have read in this book, Texas is no stranger to wild weather. Use the Internet or your library to learn more about hurricanes, tornadoes, and hailstorms that have occurred in recent years. Create a list of emergency items you may need in the event of a natural disaster. Encourage your family to assemble these items in a durable, watertight storage tub. Discuss with your family what to do if a violent storm approaches your area.

- This book talks about Texas's most amazing places. While pictures and descriptions are great starting points, there's nothing like being there in person! Where would you like to visit first? Use the Internet and other resources to learn about the place you would like to go, and make a tri-fold travel brochure about it. Include pictures, descriptions, and a map that shows someone how to get there. Share your brochure with your teacher, family, and friends.

GLOSSARY

aquifer (AH-kwuh-fuhr) A layer of underground rock that contains water.

bayou (BY-oo) A slow-moving or marshy body of water.

drought (DROWT) A long period of little or no rain.

erosion (ih-ROH-zhuhn) The act of wearing down over a long period of time, usually by weather.

escarpment (ih-SKARP-muhnt) A long cliff separating two mostly flat areas.

fertilizer (FUHR-tuh-ly-zuhr) Matter added to soil or land to make it better for growing plants.

helium (HEE-lee-uhm) A colorless gas used in balloons, lamps, and welding.

metropolitan (meh-truh-PAH-luh-tuhn) Having to do with a metropolis, which is a large and densely populated city or group of cities.

reef (REEF) A ridge of rocks or coral at or near the surface of the water.

secede (sih-SEED) To withdraw from an organization.

sorghum (SOHR-guhm) A type of grass used to make a variety of foods and to feed animals.

subtropical (suhb-TRAH-pih-kuhl) Having to do with the areas next to the warm areas near the equator.

INDEX

Due to the changing nature of Internet links, the Rosen Publishing Group, Inc., has developed an online list of websites related to the subject of this book. This site is updated regularly. Please use this link to access the list: http://www.powerkidslinks.com/sot/geo